MCR

W9-AOP-818

How Do Animals Keep Clean?

Faith Hickman Brynie

I Like READING About ANIMALS!

Contents

Note to Parents and Teachers: The *I Like Reading About Animals!* series supports the National Science Education Standards for K–4 science. The Words to Know section introduces subject-specific vocabulary words for the two different reading levels presented in this book (new reader and fluent reader), including pronunciation and definitions. Early readers may need help with these new words.

Words to Know

New Readers

antlers (ANT lurs)—Branching horns on moose, antelope, or deer.

breaching (BREECH ing)—Jumping above the water's surface.

grooming (GROO ming)—Cleaning or brushing.

Fluent Readers

community (kuh MYOO nuh tee)—A group of animals or plants living together.

energy (EN ur gee)—The power that people and animals use to be active.

gland—A small sac under the skin that makes oil.

parasite (PAR uh syt)—A creature that lives on or in another living thing and takes energy from it.

pollen (PAH lun)—Fine, powdery material in flowers.

predator (PREH duh tur)—An animal that hunts and eats other animals.

preen—To clean feathers with a beak or a tongue.

KEEPING CLEAN

Do you want to get clean? Hop in the shower! This penguin is standing in a waterfall. It is like a shower for the penguin. This is one way to keep clean.

How do animals keep clean?

Animals clean their bodies in many ways. Birds preen themselves. They use their beaks to get dirt and insects out of their feathers.

Some animals clean one another. They clean each other's fur or feathers with their tongue, beak, claws, or paws.

What other ways do animals keep clean? Let's find out!

What is this lion doing?

The lion is licking its paw. His tongue has bumps. ▷
The tongue works like a brush. It gets dirt off the
lion's body. It brushes the lion's fur, too.

Why do cats lick themselves and one another?

Lions and other cats spend a lot of time
licking their fur. They lick their bodies to take
off dirt and wastes that may stick to them
when they hunt and eat.

Mother lions and other cats lick their
babies, too. Licking babies does more than
clean them. It is one of the many ways that
the mother and the cub know that they should
stay together.

What is grooming?

One chimp is cleaning another chimp. It is picking bugs out of its hair. The cleaning is called **grooming**. Many animals groom each other. The grooming helps them stay friends.

Why do chimps groom one another?

When they are relaxing, chimps often groom themselves or one another. They use one hand to push back the hair. Then they use the other hand or their lips or teeth to pick away dirt, leaves, or dead skin.

Grooming does more than keep chimps clean. Chimps live together in a group. The group is called a community. Grooming helps members of a community live together peacefully.

Is this eel going to eat the shrimp?

No. The eel opens its mouth. Here comes a cleaner shrimp! The shrimp cleans the eel's mouth. It cleans more than dirt. It eats tiny animals that live on the eel.

What do cleaner shrimps do?

Cleaner shrimps eat parasites on fish and eels. Parasites are living things that get their energy from the animal they live on. The moray eel has parasites in its mouth. The shrimp eats the parasites.

Many fish depend on cleaner shrimps to get rid of parasites. The fish often swim in front of the shrimps to ask for cleaning.

Why does a hoverfly clean itself?

This hoverfly (HUH vur fly) cleans its head, mouth, and wings. Cleaning its eyes helps it see better. Cleaning its wings helps it fly better.

What do hoverflies gain from cleaning themselves?

Cleaning helps the hoverfly in many ways. Removing dirt helps the fly see, hear, taste, touch, and smell better.

Cleaning gets more food for hoverflies, too. When they visit flowers to gather **pollen**, some of it sticks to tiny hairs on their head and wings. When they clean themselves, they get the pollen grains in their mouth. They eat the pollen, so no food goes to waste.

What is this bird doing?

This blue-tailed pitta is cleaning its nest. Do you see the white bag? The bird puts wastes in the bag. The bird will fly away with the bag.

Why do birds clean their nests?

The blue-tailed pitta is like many birds. It flies from the nest carrying a white, jelly-like bag. It drops the bag far from the nest. The bag is full of body waste.

Taking feces away from the nest does two important things. First, it keeps the nest dry and clean. Second, it gets rid of smells that could attract predators.

How do elephants get clean?

◀ The elephant is taking a bath. It uses its trunk as a hose. It sucks up water, then sprays it. The elephant gets cool and clean at the same time!

Are elephants water animals?

African elephants are the heaviest of all land animals. Their size does not keep them out of the water, though. Bathing helps elephants stay clean and comfortable.

Elephants love water, and they swim well. Herds of wild elephants look for ponds and rivers where they can bathe. During the dry season when water is hard to find, elephants dig holes in riverbeds until they hit water.

What is on this caterpillar?

This caterpillar is covered in wax. Its skin makes the wax. The wax helps keep the caterpillar clean. It helps it stay healthy, too.

What does wax do for insects?

This atlas moth caterpillar makes long strings of wax that stick to its body. The wax may block parasites. A parasite could cause disease in the caterpillar. Some insect parasites lay their eggs in caterpillars. When the eggs hatch, they kill the caterpillar. If a parasite tries to lay its eggs in this caterpillar, the wax will stop it.

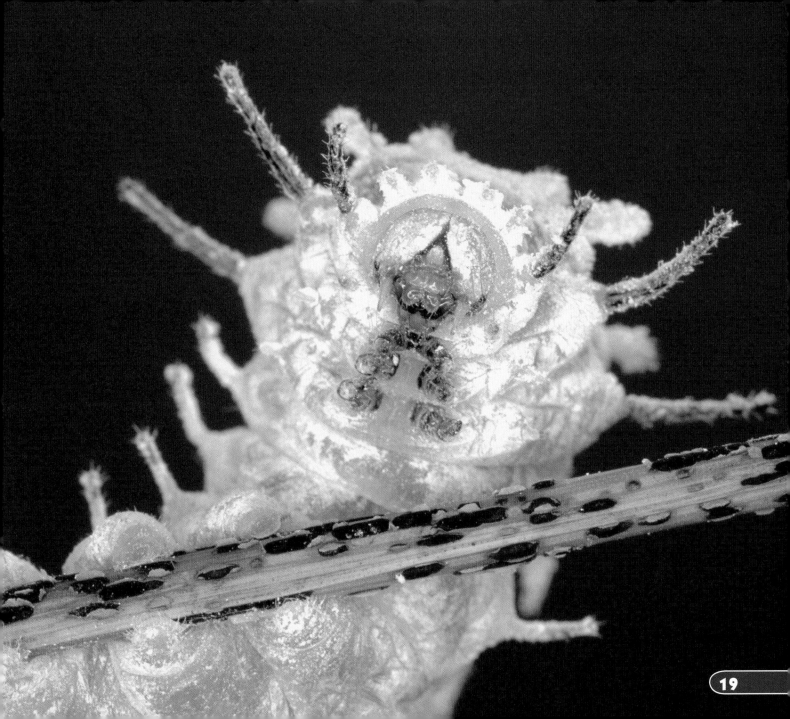

Why is this zebra rolling in the dust?

Is this zebra getting dirty? No! It is getting clean. This zebra is taking a dust bath. Zebras take dust baths almost every day.

What good is a dust bath?

As strange as it seems, zebras roll around in the dirt to get clean. The dust gets insects out of their hair. The bath rubs away dry skin and loose hair. Zebras also shake, rub, and scratch to get clean.

Zebras groom one another. Often a zebra mother grooms her baby. The grooming cleans the animals and creates a family bond between them.

What is breaching?

This humpback whale is **breaching**. Breaching means jumping out of the water. Breaching cleans the whale's skin.

How does breaching clean a whale?

When a whale breaches, it leaps above the surface of the water headfirst. It then lands on its back or belly with a big splash.

No one is sure why whales breach. They may be sending messages to other whales. But cleaning is probably important, too. Whales get barnacles (BAR nuh kulz) and lice on their skin. Breaching probably helps remove those parasites.

Are these fish chasing this turtle?

Fish are all around the green turtle. They are not chasing it. They are cleaning it. They eat tiny plants on the turtle's shell.

How do the fish and turtle help each other?

Cleaning is so important to the green turtle that it swims to a special place to find the fish. The brown surgeonfish and the yellow tangs wait there at the "cleaning station."

Cleaning tiny plants off the turtle's shell prevents diseases. And the fish get a meal in return for their cleaning services. All the animals win!

What is this moose doing?

Fuzzy skin covers the bull moose's **antlers**. The bull moose rubs its antlers on a tree. Rubbing takes off the skin. ▶

Why does the moose rub off the fuzzy velvet skin?

Velvet is soft, fuzzy skin. It covers the antlers of a bull (male) moose every summer. The antlers would not grow without the velvet. The velvet contains blood vessels that supply food to the growing antlers.

The bull rubs off the velvet in the fall when the antlers stop growing. He eats the velvet, then polishes his antlers on a tree. Polishing makes them hard, strong weapons. He uses his antlers to fight other bulls and win a mate.

How do birds clean their feathers?

This swan is preening. It preens with its bill. Preening cleans the feathers. Preening straightens out the feathers.

What are swans doing when they preen?

Swans spend a lot of time in the water. They also spend a lot of time preening their feathers. Preening gets dirt and insects out of their feathers. It keeps the feathers smooth and straight, which helps the swan swim and fly better.

Swans have a gland at the base of their tail. The gland makes oil. When preening, the swan takes oil from the gland and rubs it on the feathers. Instant waterproofing!

Learn More

Books

Sayre, April Pulley. *Splish! Splash! Animal Baths*. Minneapolis: Millbrook Press, 2000.

Souza, D. M. *Look What Mouths Can Do*. Minneapolis: Lerner, 2007.

Stewart, Melissa. *Birds*. New York: Children's Press, 2001.

Web Sites

National Geographic Kids. *Animals*. http://kids.nationalgeographic.com/animals

Yahoo! Kids. *Kids Study Animals*. http://kids.yahoo.com/animals

Index

Special thanks to Dr. Alan Kemp, Naturalists and Nomads, Menlo Park, South Africa, and Dr. David Kendall, Kendall Bioresearch Services, Bristol, England, for their expert assistance.

Enslow Elementary, an imprint of Enslow Publishers, Inc.

Enslow Elementary® is a registered trademark of Enslow Publishers, Inc.

Library of Congress Cataloging-in-Publication Data

Brynie, Faith Hickman, 1946–
    How do animals keep clean? / Faith Hickman Brynie.
      p. cm. — (I like reading about animals!)
    Includes bibliographical references and index.
    Summary: "Leveled reader that explains how different animals groom and keep clean in both first grade text and third grade text"—Provided by publisher.
    ISBN 978-0-7660-3330-6
    1. Grooming behavior in animals—Juvenile literature. I. Title.
    QL760.B79 2010
    591.56'3—dc22
                           2008050057

ISBN-13: 978-0-7660-3750-2 (paperback)

Printed in the United States of America

112009 Lake Book Manufacturing, Inc., Melrose Park, IL

10 9 8 7 6 5 4 3 2 1

To Our Readers: We have done our best to make sure all Interne Addresses in this book were active and appropriate when we wer to press. However, the author and the publisher have no control ov and assume no liability for the material available on those Interne sites or on other Web sites they may link to. Any comments or suggestions can be sent by e-mail to comments@enslow.com or t the address on the back cover.

♻ Enslow Publishers, Inc., is committed to printing our books on recycled paper. The paper in every book contains 10% to 30% post-consumer waste (PCW). The cover board on the outside of each book contains 100% PCW. Our goal is to do our part to help young people and the environment too!

Photo Credits: Photos by naturepl.com: © Andy Sands, p. 12, © Anup Shah, pp. 1, 6, 8; © David Fleetham, p. 22; © David Kja p. 13; © Doug Perrine, pp. 11, 23, 24, 25; © Francois Savigny, p. 7; © Ingo Arndt, pp. 5, 18, 19; © Jean E. Roche, p. 28; © Mike Wilkes, p. 21; © Richard Du Toit, p. 17; © Solvin Zankl, p. 4; © Staffan Widstrand, pp. 26, 27; © Thoswan Devakul, p. 15; © Tony Heald, pp. 16, 20, 32. **Photo by Shutterstock,** pp. 2–3, 30–31.

Cover Photo: © Anup Shah/naturepl.com

Series Science Consultant:
Helen Hess, PhD
Professor of Biology
College of the Atlantic
Bar Harbor, ME

Series Literacy Consultant:
Allan A. De Fina, PhD
Dean, College of Education/Professor of Literacy Education
New Jersey City University
Past President of the New Jersey Reading Association

Enslow Elementary
an imprint of

Enslow Publishers, Inc.
40 Industrial Road
Box 398
Berkeley Heights, NJ 07922
USA
http://www.enslow.com